Color God's Simple Gifts

Linda Spivey

HARVEST HOUSE PUBLISHERS
EUGENE, OREGON

COLOR GOD'S SIMPLE GIFTS

Artwork copyright © 2017 by Linda Spivey, license granted by Penny Lane Publishing, Inc.
Published by Harvest House Publishers
Eugene, Oregon 97408
www.harvesthousepublishers.com

ISBN 978-0-7369-7065-5 (pbk.)

Printed in the United States of America

19 20 21 22 23 24 25 / CM-CD / 10 9 8 7 6 5 4 3 2

A Good Place to Begin

This coloring book is for artists of all ages and talents, and that means you! Let your creative spirit free, choose any color you like, and make each beautiful image your own. There are no rules except to have fun.

Enjoy the process. Feel free to use colored pencils, pens, watercolors, markers, and crayons—or any combination—to add color and texture to each design. Notice that all the pictures are printed on just one side of the paper. To keep colors from bleeding through to the next page, simply slip an extra piece of paper underneath the page you're working on. When finished, you might like to remove the page from the book, trim it to size, and frame your artwork for all to see.

Most importantly, have fun with the process. Enjoy experimenting with contrasting colors or different shades of the same color. Try lighter hues for a softer look, or layer and blend your colors for even more options. Allow some white space or saturate the entire piece with rich, vibrant color, depending on your mood. Let your worries go, relax in the moment, and allow your creative spirit to lead the way!

Every Good and Perfect

Gift

Is from Above

Coming Down from the

FATHER

of the Heavenly Lights

James 1:17

God Is the One Who Provides

2 Corinthians 9:10

Seed to the Farmer

Bread to Eat

Give all your worries and cares to God, for He cares about you! 1 Peter 5:7

FAITH HOPE LOVE

LOVE

The Greatest of
These Is
LOVE

— 1 Corinthians 13:13 —

The LORD Is GOOD and His Love Endures Forever

Psalm 100:5

Think on These Things

THE
PEACE
OF
GOD
WILL BE WITH YOU

Philippians 4:8-9

Whatever is True, Noble and Just,
Whatever is Pure, Lovely and of Good Report,
Anything Praiseworthy

The HEAVENS Declare The GLORY of GOD The SKIES proclaim The WORK Of His HANDS

PSALM 19:1

Take Delight in the LORD and He will give you the desires of Your Heart

PSALM 37:4

My GOD

Will meet all your needs according to the riches of His glory in Christ Jesus

Philippians 4:19

Those Who Let GOD Provide Will ALWAYs Be Satisfied

The Morning Hour Has Gold in Hand

This Is the Day the Lord Has Made

In the morning, O Lord, you hear my voice;
In the morning I lay my requests before
you and *wait Expectantly.* Psalm 5:3

He
Has made
Everything Beautiful
in Its Time
Ecclesiastes 3:11

Sometimes
the SIMPLEST
Things
Are the
Best

BE THANKFUL

Everything God Created Is Good

1 Timothy 4:4

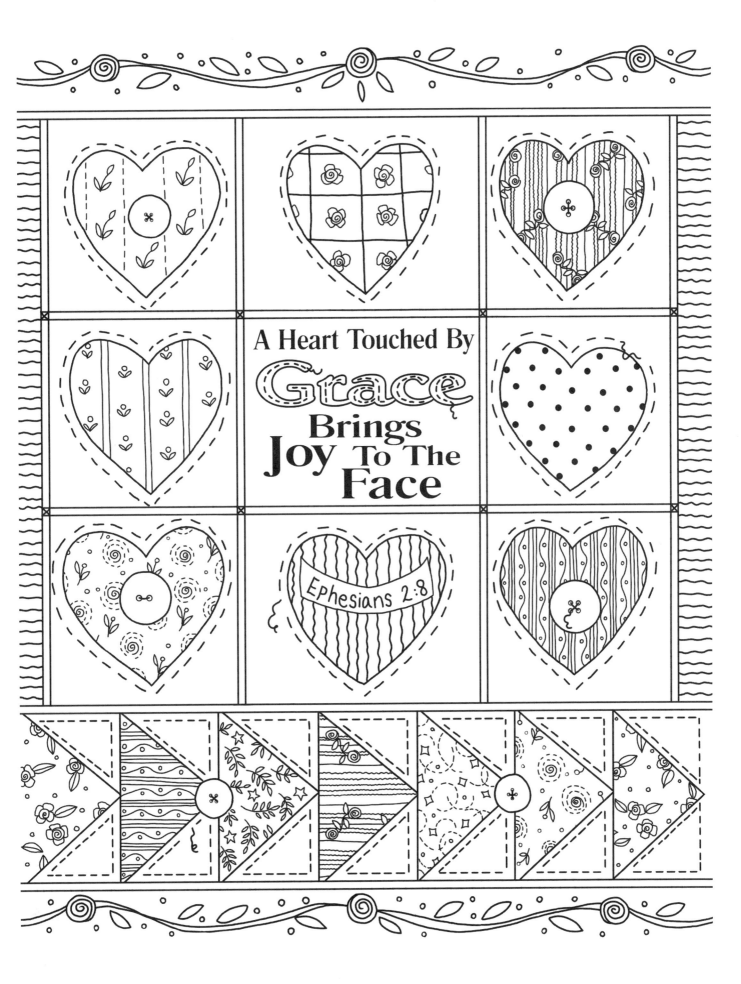

A Heart Touched By
Grace
Brings
Joy To The
Face

Ephesians 2:8

The real Secret of
Happiness
is not what you give or what
you receive, but what
you *Share*

Where Your Treasure Is

Matthew 6:21

There Your Heart Will Be Also

God Shows Kindness By

Filling Our Hearts With

JOY

Binding Crops In Their Season

Giving Rain From Heaven

Acts 14:17

Providing Plenty Of Food

KINDNESS
When Given Away...
Keeps Coming Back

Plant Kindness ~ Gather Love

Give, and it will be
Given to you....
with the measure you use,
it will be measured
to you.

Luke 6:38

A Beautiful Memory Is a *Treasure*

Love

Be *Still* and know that **I AM GOD**

Lead
A
Quiet Life

Let ALL that I am wait Quietly
before God, for my **HOPE**
is in **HIM**...my *Rock and my Salvation!*

Psalm 62:5-6

The Earth Is
Full of the Goodness of the
LORD
Psalm 33:5

Enjoy Today—It Won't Be Back

Great Is Thy Faithfulness

Your Mercies Are NEW Every Morning

— Lamentations 3:23 —

1 Timothy 6:17

Put your HOPE in GOD, who richly provides us with Everything for our enjoyment.

The Faithful *Love* of the LORD **Never Ends!** *His Mercies Never Cease*

Lamentations 3:22

FAITH

Worry
Ends Where
Faith Begins

— 1 Peter 5:7 —

My Job Is To Take Care Of The Possible And Trust GOD With The Impossible

Matthew 19:26

Trust In The Lord

With All Your Heart

And Lean NOT On

Your Own Understanding

In GOD We TRUST

Proverbs 3:5

Linda Spivey's country style of painting reflects what she loves…old crocks and baskets, weathered wood, and cracked flower pots. She often uses Scripture verses and simple poems to reflect the ideas she values most. Her art is a popular choice for home product designs and appears in her books *Family, Grandchildren, Friends* and *Baby: A Gift of Memories.*

For information on more Harvest House coloring books for adults, please visit our website:
www.harvesthousepublishers.com